Knock Up
Parable

from here to beyond

Ashish Shekhar

pencil

ISBN 978-93-5559-147-0
© Ashish Shekhar 2021
Published in India 2021 by Pencil

A brand of

One Point Six Technologies Pvt. Ltd.
123, Building J2, Shram Seva Premises,
Wadala Truck Terminal, Wadala (E)
Mumbai 400037, Maharashtra, INDIA
E connect@thepencilapp.com
W www.thepencilapp.com

DISCLAIMER: *The opinions expressed in this book are those of the authors and do not purport to reflect the views of the Publisher.*

Author biography

My Parents named me Ashish, and I added my father's name to it, Shekhar, so people call me Ashish Shekhar. I am an ambivert who believes in creativity and looks for art and opportunities in places people seldom think of. I live in Mumbai. A city that sets me free, and I couldn't ask more from life. In me, you can find every caste and race, every color, and every face. Writing, singing, and filmmaking are ingrained in me, so my life is characterized by rhymes, angles, melody, themes, and tunes. I believe nothing is impossible as far as you are putting all your heart and mind into it and by that one can do anything they want in life. My concepts stem from the situations I sometimes put myself into. One can follow me on Instagram calmly_calloff and my blog Bespectacled Hummer on WordPress.

CONTENTS

The Ghost

I don't reckon people come back after they go into the
afterlife,
But that sound I heard from the kitchen,
The constant sound of chomping
That spine chilling unseen touch
That latched door kept getting unlatched
Those visible feet from behind the curtain
And, the chasing face I see through the car's convex mirror
And, that running sound I hear from the other room
Something keeps scenting like soul-stirring memories
Made me think
Is that you up for the payback?
who is blowing me for not fulfilling your obsession,
Is that you who is here to take me with you?
staring into my phone while I am typing this,
Is that you who isn't gone from my life?
who came along with me from the graveyard,
Is that you who couldn't take rejections?
who don't believe some people kill when their dignity gets
threatened,
Is that you who still doesn't understand? No means no.

GOD IS A WOMAN

Women's existence must be a priority, but we won't prioritize them unless a specific occasion drops on our calendar. Apart from 'Women's day' and other festivities, we treat them like machines we take for granted. Their rights are often dealt with in an inferior manner. It's a known fact that women strive hard at everything they do and put a lot of effort without expecting any attention while maintaining an equilibrium amid an ocean of things, yet they do not get the love they deserve. Let us wash our sins and bathe in the power of wisdom that women can spin your world around and around depending on how you treat her. This message should be broadcast loud and clear, especially to people who think that women are feeble. Our folklore cautions us that they can don the avatar of various goddesses such as Saraswati – the one who parts knowledge, Laxmi – the one who showers love and wealth – and god forbid, she can become the evil-finisher Kali when lines are crossed.

Men come from women, and women are from heaven. They keep you in her womb for months, knowing very well that they will face numerous difficulties and challenges to begin our journey called life. Can you imagine a scenario when a child is inside a woman's womb, but she doesn't care about you, and she will do what she wants, which could be anything - eating what she wants to, going bungee jumping, or going on a roller coaster ride? But she won't do that.

No country in the globe is bereft of the atrocities against women. Rape, acid attacks, domestic violence, eve-teasing, sexual harassment, stalking, female feticide, lack of access to education, honor killings, equal pay, early marriage, sex trafficking, objectification of women, et cetera, are unfortunately ubiquitous. Empowered women who live their lives on their terms are often labeled with names because they refuse to accept our patriarchal society's so-called norms. Men call women hussy and challenging, as they cannot explain their wrongdoings to society and instead blame women. And, a "slut" – the universal derogatory term - is a woman who refuses to rub men in the wrong way. Indeed, when they can't shut her, they try to slut her.

Remember, it all starts with ignorance towards specific cultures and mindsets which we are aware of. Despite that, we heed it because no one has the guts to challenge traditions that are unfair to women. We often forget that women are human beings, just like us. 'Men will be Men' is the most misguided and cruel phrase our society uses to defend men's wrongdoing. This has been setting a wrong precedent for years now. Forgiving a man who has done injustice to a woman unrelated to you sends a clear indication to more men like him that their atrocities against women can be buried without any hassle. The world has seen that letting men degrade women (on whose shoulder the responsibility of making the world a better place rests) has catastrophic consequences.

Domestic violence and child abuse are on the surge globally. You reap what you sow, and the seeds of toxicity that we have planted in men catch up with society. There's no way to escape this vicious circle! There are record-breaking SOS calls from across the globe from women seeking protection from abuse and violence. We have gotten to this problem because, since childhood, we have instilled in women that night trips are best avoided to shun "monsters." We forget that these monsters sometimes stay with us in our very homes. Since you let them stay with you, they'll kill everyone as it's their innate characteristic.

Most of our lives, we have flung around vulgar adages like "she's this type or that type of woman. Some people go a step further and call them mental, crazy, mad, insane, as though it's a tradition when all they are doing is speaking up for themselves. No one has ever stopped anyone from committing such offenses, as it didn't seem offensive then. But when you grow up and observe things you have always known, you gain a different perspective. Today, those words mean something; they represent the hordes of women who are carefully ignored and laughed at because society feels insecure when intellectual women surround them. We fear them and thus bully them as they seem like aliens who don't follow the so-called culture and hang their caps on it. Half of the world's women are fighting for equal rights and proving themselves as capable human beings. More stories of women being killed by their obsessive lover or burnt to death over dowry emerge every day as compared to their achievements or battles that they win because we aren't encouraging men to handle the empowered women.

The world has never been taught that women are above their bodies and appearance, reflecting the tales of many disgusting and cowardly acts of the supposed masculine men, which women want to escape but don't know how to. But, of course, atrocities against women aren't limited to any social hierarchy; they are omnipresent. It is arduous to cross over the taboo threshold that we have always thought about but never spoke against. The reason might be the commonality of the act. No one has an issue with some catcalling, but people overlook that it might end up in rape; one slap to a woman is termed passable, but the one slap could soon turn into a sequence of slaps might as well end up as domestic violence. It's one of the plethoras of issues Indian women and women globally are enduring.

It's time to change one of the cruelest mindsets we have towards women: a patriarchal legacy! It doesn't allow us to see women as human beings, but it's what they are, more than anything else. We must unlearn all the toxic thoughts that make us so insecure that men hit women and try to own them without their approval. Such mindsets can't be changed in one night, so to escape all these mayhems, I'll now be listening to 'God is a woman' by Ariana Grande because clearly, she's not treated like one.

The sharp-witted County of my Dreams

It's 2022. As we all know, it's been an unfortunate example of the horrendous activities taking place around the globe – Virus, horror against women, coups, mob lynching, corruption, honor killings, murders, natural calamities, terrorism, suicide et cetera. Some fools believe this to be the end of the world. I do not need to remind you that it's not the end of the world when things don't go the way everyone sees them. I see things like a half glass full, not empty! What's occupied the half glass, you might ask? It suffices to say a tiny ray of hope. It can be anything, praying to the almighty, getting away from reality, but mine is enormous.

A country - Yes. In situations that are literally out of my control, I tend to shift my focus towards fictitious things. So, let me take you on a ride to a place where angels exist - in people, where differences between males and females are purely biological. Here, women are not judged for their short dresses or lifestyle; men are not labeled as lesser men because they cry or are not strong enough to fight. Where pink doesn't belong to gender, but it is just a color. Here, street dogs and animals are friends, not things to play with, and the language is just a medium to communicate, not the criteria to judge intelligence, and stereotype is just a fancy word. Education is not just duty in this country but a need to grow as an independent individual; trust, honesty, truth, wisdom are not mere words, and anger, fear, and jealousy are just myths that cannot be debunked.

Imagine a place greener than the trees, land filled with food and water, people who aren't dependent on each other but live for each other, and surroundings are synonymous with ecstasy and tranquillity. My country isn't just a serene jungle but a modern world of increasing heights. Here, lands are not forcefully taken over but given to (pause) improvise the condition for the country's well-being.

This is a place where women feel much safer than the world we live in. The laws are stricter, but it was never needed to implement them because while growing up, the boys were taught that it's ok to cry and that girls and women are much more than their sexual needs. Here, values and morals are achieved in childhood, and the need to go down the wrong path is oblivion. Also, women do not need to fight for their rights because they are instilled within the constitution. They are paid equally to men.

LOVE here is true to its definition and form. I imagine my country to be free from prejudicial stereotypes. It doesn't matter who you love - the person's sex, caste, religion, or beliefs do not shake the basic and today's rare-found element of humanity. Mockery exists only in the field of entertainment, and everybody is given a chance to leave their cocoon and fly out of their mediocrity and, if otherwise - is not frowned upon. This place is obscure to the stench of gremlins lurking in the veil. Unity and strength are the long declared motto.

People communicate as if they are one big family. No pretentious grandchildren or greedy daughters-in-law exist here. Folks working as waiters and the CEO greet each other with an equal amount of respect. Unlike this world, the police are considered public servants, and arresting the accused is the only power in their jurisdiction. Here we tackle natural calamities with the advent of newer technologies, where security isn't just the iris or fingerprint scanners of devices but in our minds regarding our country. This country not only provides you with swift internet speeds but also has the resources to make travel seem like an evening walk to those who want to meet their loved ones instantly.

You see, the people of my country are downright pleasant, with a man winning a beauty pageant and a girl making their country proud by winning gold medals in sports.

Ring some bells? Because these are the predicaments of the world, we live in. We judge everyone around us and dislike it when the same thing happens to us. As mentioned earlier, the country exists just in my dreams, but why are we destroying the real ones we have? It's high time we behaved like humans, and instead of the empty title-tattle, we should be spreading humanity - it's the only thing we are left with, which some haven't even given a try. So let's make the country of our dreams by carving a path into reality!

What it is

I know what it is to wait for someone who's already in my life but has never really been there for you.
I know what it is to feel blank because you've been given everything that you once had.
I know what it is to stay quiet about the harm caused by one's own mistakes.
I know what it is to cry in front of the person you know, who will stab you in the end.

I know what it is to be judged and tagged because you often wear silence on your face.
I know what it is to hold cigarettes instead of holding someone you love.
I know what it is to get crashed for being upset about your injuries.
I know what it is to value someone without being valued.

I know what it is to live when you don't even feel alive.
I know what it is to be called names and get labeled
when all you are doing is finding ways to survive another day.
I know what it is to hold someone who is leaving you.

I know what it is when you stop loving things you once couldn't live without.

I know what it is to be seen and ignored like you don't
even exist.
I know what it is to be only left with the lullaby of your
haunting past.

15

I know what it is to walk with a heart roaringly soaked and
heavy, which moans louder than stitches.
I know what it is to sleep with betrayal's heaviness, which
feels like pain under the rib.
I know what it is to be on the beach only with sands.
I know what it is to stay on a path that leads you nowhere.

Come back

My love
My desire to live
Come
Come back to me
Tear me, fear me
but stay
This house
isn't home anymore
Tell me
You miss waking me up at midnight
for your uneasy dreams
Tell me
You want to sleep over me
and miss waking up
next to me
Tell me
You, too, feel the misery
of being apart
You miss me
when you touch yourself
Tell me
you miss me
seeing clothes
which were once
stained with sperm

Tell me
How your wounds
were comfortable
just with me
and,
None made you feel at home
Tell me
You love me
more than any solace
Come back, my love
Come back to me
Come in me
See, there is nothing left
in me
without you
It's all broken
and lost paths
Come back to see
that my heartaches
when it can't say
how much it craves you
Come back
And, melt in me again
Tell me
It feels like we
were never parted
Carry me wherever you go
Make me cry
 in your arms
Make me alive
Tell me it isn't over
And, you looked for me

in every tinder match
Tell me the face
you want to kiss
isn't there, anywhere
Tell me this time feels like
An ending hope
you don't wanna lose
Come
Come back, my love
Come back to the room
of dry leaves
and broken dreams
Come
Come and fix me
with the love
we had
since forever

Edge

that mug I
gifted you on
your birthday
now has dry
bloodstains
on its broken edges
it has not given me pain
when you hit me
out of obsession
but it has made a
wounds inside my
heart
thinking how your
whip hand over me
always kept
my life at stake
knowing I never made a
way to home
away from you

Lifetime

time has healed me
in a way that
the wound you gave
on my body
losing its mark
fading its color
merging with the skin
of my thighs
but
the mark on
heart
the love that
once came with light
has given me
burns for a
lifetime.

Choosing

Believe me, one day
you will evolve
as a winner
Become
whoever you want to
you are going to
shout out loud
your name
from the peaks
of the mountain
and, see the
magic of
being love in
yourself
magic of choosing
yourself over
everything.

Fairytale as it seems

In the dreams I see,
People that state 'we.'
Weather with boundless ski,
And the people with titchy glee.

A place full of tranquillity,
With the mortals' devotion to the only deity.
Being better at docility,
But very ingenious for gullibility.

Shadows forsaken in the daylights,
Open on outlooks but elude from fights.
Green and green it gets with the proliferating heights,
Enthralling with their quality that of the Knights.

Where wars do not prevail,
And no gremlins lurking in the veil,
Winning is just a game, and no fear of 'the fail.'
Mediocrity isn't frowned upon, where the hammers live
happily with the nail.

Modern here merely means growth,
The natives here shall stand by their oath.
Where eminence is opposed to sloth,
With the vision of a blooming story of promise.

Fairytale as it seems, it would all be feasible,
Sans the self-conscious, it seems reasonable!

23

Illusionary

It's silent
it's scary
I know this won't be
a tale of a fairy
moving out of time
forgot where
to go
This body has gone
through all the low
It's like December
Cold, freezing
and numb
Snatching all I had
even the crumb
Stitches in the heart
weren't stitched
well to carry
Place that favors my soul
is just illusionary

Goodbye

You should also give it
/a try.
I don't know how you stopped looking after
/and why,
Swallowing shattered pieces
/waiting for wounds to dry,
Pushing to move on
/hoping not to die
Maybe you have found something new
/maybe another guy,
I know you were already ready to leave
/and say goodbye.

Forced vision

He wooed her,
making her heart
alive
giving her a reason
to smile
He loved her, understood
when she needed him
and lent her his
shoulder to
vent on
He married her
and gave her a
reason to feel alive
except
it was an illusion
A brutal one
Now he gave
her a reason to end
her life
The scars scarred
her for a lifetime
How time changes
when love becomes
a forced
vision

Vowel-chime

I could turn your
one glimpse
into a never-ending vowel-chime,
Love and romance
arrive with a rarer
crime
No manipulations
Heart with so many
variations
Just wait for
your allowance-sign
To give you the world
against time.

May be

All dusk
No light
Maybe this is the battle
I have to fight
No blood
Only a broken piece
Perhaps I have only sand
even on the beach
All the forgotten
window
Sealed door
Maybe there
is no scope to roar

Shattered

Life would be easy
if there were a way
to erase the touch
of that
one person
who left us
shattered.

Prevail

You left me
on the edge of
my vulnerabilities
where
my heart
shrank
and I wanted
to die
but
I learned to
prevail
instead.

I hope

I hope someday
you lie less and
accept more
I hope someday
you pretend less
and stay uncooked
I hope in this world
full of people
selling themselves
for nothing -
you will save an untouched
corner of your
heart for your own
soul

Trust

Imagine a scenario where you are
walking on a rope -
just rope and nothing else.
And you are pretty adept at it.
So you decide to share it
with someone you trust.
And now that person is walking
on the same rope as you.
It's woggles, but you trust that person.
Suddenly,
that person cuts the rope,
and you are holding onto your life.
This is how people feel
when they are betrayed.

Delusion

Only if one day
you sit and recall
everything you have done
in your own self-proclaimed
delusional world
you will understand
what you have
served me in the
name of love

एक दफा फिर से

कि तुम आओ एक दफा फिर से

मैं कहानियां सुनाऊं

तुम बाहों में सो जाओ एक दफा फिर से !

मैं तुम्हारी गलियों के चक्कर लगाऊं

तुम छज्जे से देखने आओ

कि मैं फिर गुलाब लाऊं

तुम उन्हें छुपा के घर ले जाओ एक दफा फिर से !

मैं तोहफे में खत लिखूं

लंबी रातों को तुम्हारी गुफ्तगू सुनते खो जाऊं

कि शहर का कोई कोना ढूंढे

तुम किसी को ना आते देख मुझे चूम लो एक दफा फिर से !

मैं कस के पकड़ लूं और तुम्हें कभी जाने ना दूं

इस बार दर्द नहीं बस सुकून लाऊं

 ये उम्र कम पड़ेगी तुम्हारे साथ बिताने को

कह कर गले लगा लो एक दफा फिर से !

तुम एक उम्र लेकर आओ,

मैं पलकों पर बैठाने के इरादे

तुम फिर बिना किसी शोर के घर आओ

मैं अंदर कर तुझे कुंडी लगा लूं एक दफा फिर से !

मैं तुम्हारी तस्वीर चुरा कर अपने पास रख लूं

तुम खत में हमारे एक होने की खुशियां लिखो

तुम किसी दूर शहर पैग़ाम भेजो

 मैं तुम्हारी एक झलक देखने

दौड़ा चलाऊं एक दफा फिर से !

तुम मेरी बाहों को तकिया बनाओ

 मैं तुम्हें और करीब लाने के तरीके ढूंढूं

 उन दिसंबर की रातों में,

तुम मुझे ठंडे हाथों से छुओ

मैं तुम्हार आहों में पसीज जाऊं एक दफा फिर से !

मैं अपनी खामियों से भी इश्क कर बैठूं

तुम्हारे जाने के डर से सबसे बैर कर जाऊं

तुम ठहरने के बहाने ढूंढो

मैं तुम्हारे होने का गुरुर कर जाऊं एक दफा फिर से !

तुम सड़कों पर मेरा हाथ पकड़ लो

मैं भीड़ में तुम्हें ही ढूंढूं

आओ मैं तुम पे कोई किताब लिखूं एक दफा फिर से !

जो इश्क अधूरा रह गया, उसे अधूरा रह जाने दो

मगर साथ तुम रह जाओ

तुम पलट के मुस्कुराओ

मैं दिल लुटा बैठूं

एक दफा फिर से !

उस इश्क़ का क्या करें

जो सीने पे सर रख के सोये,

करवट पे खंजर चला दे

उस इश्क़ का क्या करें ?

जो हर शब् आगोश में आशना सा लगे,

सुबह किसी रक़ीब का हाँथ थाम ले

उस इश्क़ का क्या करें ?

जिसे तुम खुदपे कब्ज़ा करने दो,

उसपे तुम ज़रा सा हक़ ना दिखा सको

उस इश्क़ का क्या करें ?

जो अल्फाज़ो में बेपनाह इश्क़ बताये,

तुम्हरे दर्द में तुम्हे छूने भी ना आये

उस इश्क़ का क्या करें ?

जो तुम्हे गले लगा के रोये,

तुम्हरे अश्क़ो पे मु मोड़ ले

उस इश्क़ का क्या करें ?

जिसे तुम गलती से भी तकलीफ ना दे सको,

वो फरेब का लिबास ओढ़ के आये

उस इश्क़ का क्या करें ?

जिसे तुम रूह समझो,

वो तुम्हरी सारी रूहानियत ले जाये

उस इश्क़ का क्या करें ?

जो तुम्हे चुम के अपना होने का एहसास दिलाये,

महफ़िलो में जा के सबका हो जाये

उस इश्क़ का क्या करें ?

जो पानी में साथ बहे,

तूफान मे अपना किनारा कर लें

उस इश्क़ का क्या करें ?

जिसके होने का तुम दुनिया से गुर्रर करो,

वो दुनिया के सामने तुम्हे महज़ एक सरफिरा दीवाना कह

जाये

उस इश्क़ का क्या करें ?

जिसे तुम टूट कर चाहो,
वो तुम्हे तोड़ के चला जाये ,
उस इश्क़ का क्या करें?

जिसे तुम अपना रंगरेज़ मानो,
वो तुम्हरे जज़्बात पे काले बदल घेर जाये
उस इश्क़ का क्या करें?

तो आ

ये जो सन्नाटों में शोर हैं

ये जो आँखों में चुभती दुपहर हैं

ये जो आधी तेरी, आधी मेरी कहानी हैं

ये जो तू सुन सके, बुन सके तो आ !

जिस्म पे हाँथ फेरने वाले तो बोहोत हैं

जो तू इन्हे महसूस कर सके तो आ

मेरी आँखों ने धुप में अँधेरे देखें हैं

जो तू मेरी रातों मे भी उजाला कर सके तो आ

बिखरे हैं निशान तेरे

तू इनमे खुदको फिर से ढाल सके तो आ

दिल थक गया हैं, मन भर गया हैं

तू इनमे रूह दाल सके तो आ

वाक़िफ़ हूँ तेरी बादस्तूर चाहत से

जो तू मेरे इश्क़ की रूहानियत देख सके तो आ

मैं ख़ानाबदोश सा, बेजान सा हूँ

तू जो मुझे घर कर सके तो आ

मैं बेरंग सा, काली स्याही से मेरे अल्फ़ाज़

जो तू मेरा रंगरेज़ बन सके तो आ

इश्क़ तेरा भी हैं, मेरा भी हैं

तू इसे हमारा कर सके तो आ

क्या से क्या हो जाता हूँ

मैं सपनो में भी रंग जाता हूँ,
ना जाने क्या से क्या हो जाता हूँ

लिख दे तू मेरी भी किस्मत अपने ढंग से,
मैं लिखने जाता हूँ तोह अल्फ़ाज़ भूल जाता हूँ
कोई लकीर खींच दे, मुझे मेरी हदें बता दे,
तुझे देख के मैं देहलीजें लाँघ जाता हूँ

मैं सपनो में भी रंग जाता हूँ,
ना जाने क्या से क्या हो जाता हूँ

सोने दे मुझे अपने सीने पे,
बिस्तर पे मैं सिलवटों में फस जाता हूँ
चुम लून तेरी आँखों को,
जो मुझे देखती हैं तो मैं मुक़म्मल हो जाता हूँ

मैं सपनो में भी रंग जाता हूँ,

ना जाने क्या से क्या हो जाता हूँ

मेरा हक़ बता दे मुझे,

मैं जताता हूँ तो तेरे सरे ग़मों को अपना कह जाता हूँ

यु तो रास्तों में भटका हूँ,

पर तुझ तक जाती हर मोड़ पहचान जाता हूँ

मैं सपनो में भी रंग जाता हूँ,

ना जाने क्या से क्या हो जाता हूँ

तुझे ओढ़ के,

मैं खुदसे ही बेईमान सा हो जाता हूँ

मैं सपनो मे भी रंग जाता हूँ,

ना जाने क्या से क्या हो जाता हूँ

वो जो

वो जो मोहब्बत में तुझसे करता हूं
वो अगर तुझे भी हो जाए
तो क्या बात हो जाए

वो जो मैं जमाने से इंतजार में हूं
वो खबर तुझ तक पहुंच जाए
तो क्या बात हो जाए

वो जो मुझे मुझसे ले गएं हैं
वो खुद को भी मुझे दे जाएं
तो क्या बात हो जाए

कबतक

चलो ज़िन्दगी की तरफ चलते हैं
कबतक ये बिखरे रिश्तों को समेटते रहेंगे,

चलो खोये रास्तों को , खुद ही ढूंढते हैं
कबतक किसी का इंतज़ार करते रहेंगे

जो चला गया उसे गुज़र जाने देतें हैं ,
कबतक उमीदों का मातम मानते रहेंगे

वक़्त

समेट ले तू कुछ लोगो को इस बार
वक़्त बुरा हैं,
अपने पेहचान्ने मे आसानी होगी!

बदनसीब

मेरी उलझी रंजिशों का कसूरवार

तुझे मानु या खुदको

जो सब लूटा बैठा तुझपे,

बदनसीब उसको मानु या तुझको

चेहरा

जो मैं इल्ज़ाम लगाने वालो से मु मोड़ भी लून

तो इस बात से कैसे मु मोड़ लून की

उनमे एक चेहरा तू भी था!

सड़क

फरेब का इनके कोई तोड़ नहीं हैं

कौड़िओ की सीरत लिए

अपनी ही नज़रो में गिरे हैं

झूठ की सड़क इनकी

सच की तरफ जाती कोई मोड़ नहीं हैं

कतल

क़िस्सा कहानी बने से पहले ही ख़तम हो गया

में एक तरफ़ा इश्क़ में था कतल हो गया

फरेब

वो तूफ़ान के बाद आता है

में हमसफ़र समझ लेता हूँ

वो फिर कोई फरेब ले के आता है

में लौटा हुआ इश्क़ समझ लेता हूँ

बाकी है

उसे देख के

उसको पाने की चाह अभी बाकी है

जो बरसो बाद मेरे शहर में लौटा है

उसे हुआ वो

पहला इश्क़ अभी बाकि है